From the Small Business *Primer Series*

I0468057

ENTREPRENEUR!

Can I Be One?

by

Bob Foster

Contact: bob@bobfoster.biz

Website: www.bobfoster.biz

Cover design by Dhyana Kearly www.dhyzen.com

ENTREPRENEUR! – *Can I Be One?*

Table of Contents

Books by Bob

The Primer Series:

Entrepreneur! — *Can I Be One?* (Print and Kindle)

Small Business Planning: How to Plan — Without Writing a Business Plan (Print and Kindle)

Small Business Bootstrapping: And Other Alternative Ways to Finance Your Small Business (Print and Kindle)

Small Business Financial Statements: What They Are, How to Understand Them, and How to Use Them (Print and Kindle)

Other Books:

Business Survival Reality: The Mystery of Business Births and Deaths in the U.S. (Free ebook: download from this website http://bizmaverickblog.com)

Business Ideas Book. (This ebook is scheduled for publication in mid 2016)

Be Your Own Turnaround Manager: A Common Sense Guide to Managing a Business Crisis (Currently out of print while working on second edition. For first edition — contact Bob Foster.)

All *Primer Series* books available at Amazon.com and other booksellers.

Preface

This book does *NOT* attempt to tell you how to start a business—but it does give you the information you need to determine whether or not you *SHOULD* start a business.

Each year around 6 Million[1] new full-time businesses are started in the U.S. and ....

Most of them quickly fail!

There are many very specific reasons being bantered around today as to why these businesses fail, but the underlying reason is almost always because the founder(s) did not fully understand what all is required to be an entrepreneur.

Entrepreneurship is a demanding taskmaster and every business owner, and aspiring entrepreneur, should know what will likely be required of them.

That is why this book should be read by anyone who is thinking about starting a business, as well as those who have started a business and are now realizing that being an entrepreneur is not at all what they thought it would be like.

Although this book is directed primarily at people who either are, or want to become, full time entrepreneurs, the information presented also applies to the part time "side-hustle" entrepreneur.

Entrepreneurship is not for everyone, and before you make the decision to become an entrepreneur you need to know what you're getting yourself into... and if that is what you really want to do.

It is the intention of this book to help you make that decision — so let's get started!

(1) *The complete report titled **"Business Survival Reality"** is updated annually in early summer, and can be accessed from the RH column of bizmaverickblog.com*

1 • Introduction

"Entrepreneurial capitalism is the strongest force possible for unleashing human potential." — Tom Peters

Obviously a very profound statement—and one that I agree with… for many people! By that, I mean not everyone is cut out to be an entrepreneur, and those folks who aren't need to follow other paths toward unleashing their human potential.

It appears there are way too many people who believe becoming an entrepreneur is a very simple matter—they have a "just do it" mentality. This is very likely the major contributing factor to the extremely high incidence of business failures every year (see the *Business Survival Reality* report located at bizmaverickblog.com.

There are many popular business books out today telling readers how easy it is to become an entrepreneur. If you believe everything you read, you can start a business for $100, and only work 4 hours per week.

Unfortunately, this kind of information contributes greatly to the confusion surrounding the entire concept of being an entrepreneur.

That is likely one of the reasons I frequently receive questions, like this:

~ What is an Entrepreneur—really?

~ Why should I want to be an entrepreneur?

~ Can just anyone be an entrepreneur?

~ Can I become an entrepreneur?

~ What if I fail?

~ What do I have to do to become an entrepreneur?

At the same time, even considering all the confusion and misinformation floating around about becoming an entrepreneur, we also hear these statistics:

—72% of employees say they want to quit their jobs and become entirely independent.

—61% of employees say they are likely to quit their jobs within 2 years.

It's obvious that many people—perhaps yourself—who are interested in the entrepreneurial life, just don't quite know what it is, or how to obtain it.

To make matters worse, there is even a huge difference of opinion throughout the business community, as well as the U.S. government, as to the definition of "entrepreneur."

In addition, if the latest research (see the *Business Survival Reality* report previously mentioned) is any indication, there are millions of people starting businesses every year that know very little about being an entrepreneur—and their business fails.

That's why I wrote this book. I want us to look into finding a *real* definition of an entrepreneur, and then to answer the above questions — as well as many others.

Although anyone can start a business, those with certain characteristics and knowledge will have an easier time of becoming successful.

I've provided a "test" in Chapter 8 that you can take to see where you need to strengthen your personal characteristics and business knowledge before trying to start a business.

Also, there is a "secret" to being a successful entrepreneur, and I think we should look at this secret at some length. After you learn about this secret you may not even want to become an entrepreneur. But, that's up to you.

We'll also look into the specific worlds of the "Internet Entrepreneur" and the "Home Business Entrepreneur"... two of the most active areas of entrepreneurship today.

For inspiration, I've included a chapter on "Famous Entrepreneurs" who started with little more than an idea and became hugely successful.

Then, to cap it all off, there is a chapter on "Entrepreneurial Quotes" to give you a little more inspiration.

2•What is an Entrepreneur?

"Just what is an *Entrepreneur*—really?" I receive this question periodically and I always hate to tell that person... *no one knows!*

Everyone has an opinion, but few people can agree on a common definition of "entrepreneur." This results in ongoing controversy and mixed responses to the needs of new, or aspiring, entrepreneurs.

Entrepreneur is a term being applied today to many different enterprises and disciplines. We now have a number of entrepreneurial titles, such as: Business Entrepreneur, Social Entrepreneur, Digital Entrepreneur, Lifestyle Entrepreneur, Political Entrepreneur, Moral Entrepreneur, and on, and on. Who knows what kind of entrepreneur will be named next.

Unfortunately, the word entrepreneur has been so overused and misused that it has become trite and somewhat meaningless. We badly need a new term to replace "entrepreneur"—perhaps even an entirely new Lexicon for the world of small business.

But, until that happens, as far as I'm concerned, and this book is concerned, there is only one real "entrepreneur"—the *Business* Entrepreneur! So let's take a hard look at that definition.

A Real Definition of "Entrepreneur"

Various dictionaries provide their definition of entrepreneur, and untold numbers of articles, blogs, and web sites provide a variety of definitions. Unfortunately, they are all mired down in controversy.

The famous economist, Joseph Schumpeter, maintained that unless you were starting a highly innovative, fast-growing business you were not an entrepreneur—you were simply self-employed. Many elitist business experts today follow Schumpeter's definition.

The *Economist* magazine recently mentioned a study by the *Research Institute of Industrial Economics* that said the entrepreneurial vigor of a country should be measured by the number of Billionaire entrepreneurs it had. (*Number of Billionaire entrepreneurs?... REALLY?*)

Even the government can't seem to decide on a definition—they actually offer a 45-page document just trying to define a small business. http://1.usa.gov/1JPQWo6

A great number of business "experts," gurus, and pundits believe you can't be an entrepreneur unless you have employees. Just follow some of the *LinkedIn* small business groups for a while and you'll see what I mean.

It gets worse!

U.S. government agencies, like the *U.S. Bureau of the Census*, the *Small Business Administration*, the *Bureau of Labor Statistics*, and others also believe you must have employees in order to be a real business, and they give short shrift to those businesses without employees... the majority of American businesses.

Approximately 83% (28 Million) of all U.S. businesses do NOT have employees, and I believe that every one of these business owners should be considered an entrepreneur. Oh, and this group also contributes a *Trillion* dollars a year to America's GDP.

So, all things considered—just what is a meaningful definition of "entrepreneur?"

I obviously disagree with the business elitists, and the U.S. government. I also think the definition of an entrepreneur should be simple and straightforward. So, in this book we will define an "entrepreneur" as follows:

An entrepreneur is a person who, with considerable initiative, organizes and operates a business enterprise for the primary purpose of monetary gain, while taking on greater than normal financial risk in order to do so.

This is the broad definition we'll use from here on, and I believe every shop owner; every market vendor; every home business; and every non-employee business in the world fulfills the above definition and deserves to be called *"Entrepreneur."*

Let's look at a couple of different business situations:

First, let's consider the person who starts a small business to support their minimalist lifestyle and are content with a modest income, without any high-growth expectations.

Second, is the person who cannot be satisfied, or feel fully successful, until they have rapidly grown their business into a large company worth millions of dollars and employs hundreds of people... preferably a public company.

The results, the resources, and the effort required in these two examples are worlds apart—but do these two examples fit into the above definition? Of course, but the entrepreneurs in these two examples obviously have far different characteristics, passions, and goals.

The Reluctant Entrepreneur

We should also be aware that there are certain people who may not want to be an entrepreneur at all, but are forced into it. This group could include artists, life coaches, authors, certain health care individuals, spiritual leaders, freelancers, and the like.

Entrepreneurship is usually forced on these individuals and the activity of making their profession into a "business" is a necessary evil, rather than their primary desire. Also, some of these folks may not totally fulfill our previous definition of an entrepreneur, because monetary gain may not be their primary purpose.

Unfortunately, our society forces those in this group to perform many of the functions of entrepreneurship and they reluctantly become a part of the business world. As a result, they all must understand business planning, marketing and sales, managing cash flow, understanding financial statements, and the like.

And for some, they are faced with hiring and managing employees.

However, this group does have some alternatives, such as:

~ If they are well funded, they can hire someone else to manage all the entrepreneurial stuff.

~ They can become an employee of an established business and not have to worry about the business side of their creative endeavors.

~ In some cases they may be able to join a co-op or similar organization, and rely on someone else in the group to manage the business of the group.

I'm sure that most, if not all, of the people in this group need to earn money from their endeavors. It's just that the business stuff can get in the way of their real passions... entrepreneurship is secondary.

But then—why should *anyone* want to be an entrepreneur in the first place? Let's tackle that question in the next chapter.

3•Why Be An Entrepreneur?

After satisfying a definition for entrepreneur, the next question is usually: "Why would I want to become an entrepreneur?" I think this question is best answered by Carl J. Schramm, former President and CEO of the *Kauffman Foundation*. Here is what he said:

> *"I can take control of my life. I can make my own life better. I can expand my human dignity, and I can take my fellow citizens along into the future that we can create."*
>
> —Carl J. Schramm, PhD

This message and this thought just might be the foundation upon which all small-business owners should approach the starting and running of their business. The above is usually why we become entrepreneurs.

Also, if your life has been turned upside down, for whatever reason, now might be a good time to take stock of your career—and your life. Entrepreneurship could be a part of your future.

Maybe you're one of the 72% of employees who want to quit their jobs and become independent—to know the feeling of *freedom.*

Control of Your Life

This is a feeling that no one other than another entrepreneur can describe. When you decide to become an entrepreneur you are taking control of your life, and what you choose to do with it. To many, that is called "freedom."

At the same time, the typical entrepreneur gives up much of their *physical* freedom. There is no starting time, and no quitting time... you usually start as early as physically possible, and stop when you are too tired to go on.

You may miss time with family and friends. There may be few opportunities for date night, or attending your kid's school activities. You will ask yourself many, many times why you ever wanted to be an entrepreneur.

Toby Thomas, CEO of *EnSite Solutions*, puts it this way in his analogy comparing an entrepreneur to a guy riding a lion:

> *People look at him and think; 'This guy's really got it together! He's brave!' And the man riding the lion is thinking; 'How the hell did I get on a lion, and how do I keep from getting eaten'?*
> — Toby Thomas

Sure, being an entrepreneur is scary, and very hard work, but if you have the right personal characteristics you will carry on in spite of all the fears and sacrifices, because you know you have control of your life. You will have no boss telling you what you MUST do. You will have control over your destiny — the future you are building now.

Obviously, there is much to consider before you give up your job and start to move toward entrepreneurship. Even if you have lost your job, you need to do some soul-searching before you make the commitment to become an entrepreneur.

Be sure that you are not just running away from a tough job situation... it is important that you are running toward your dream.

Although I provided this quote previously, I want to leave you with this thought:

> *Entrepreneurial capitalism is the strongest force possible for unleashing human potential.*
>
> — Tom Peters

Everyone reading these words has potential — real human potential. When you're ready to unleash that potential, consider this quotation by Tom Peters.

4•The Age and Education Myth

If you listen to current wisdom provided by business experts and pundits of the day, you will believe that in order to become a successful entrepreneur you need to be between the ages of 20 and 34—with a degree from a renowned university, preferably with an MBA.

Not True! Data from the *Kauffman Index of Startup Activity* tells us that the 20 to 34 age group has been the LEAST likely to start a business in recent years.

Conversely, the group between the ages of 55 and 64 has continued to increase in entrepreneurial activity at a rate greater than all other age groups during the past 10 years.

There is no data available for entrepreneurial activity of people over the age of 64, but if you check out a few business forums and "Senior" magazines you will discover that the entrepreneurial spirit is alive and well long past age 64.

The same is true for entrepreneurs under the age of 20. The *Kauffman Foundation* even sponsors special programs for teen entrepreneurs. There are also more and more articles and online chatter about teen entrepreneurs. So, teens—bring it on!

Education Requirements

Another bit of information presented by the *Kauffman Index* is that people with the LEAST formal education start the most businesses. This has been the situation since Kauffman's Index was started. So, don't think you need to go to college in order to start a business.

Yes, in order to become a *successful* entrepreneur you will need to have a sound understanding of how businesses work, and how you need to prepare yourself to become an entrepreneur.

But, all the education and knowledge you will likely need in order to get your business started can be found at the Library; online; and in Adult Education Classes.

You do need basic business knowledge, but all too often, formal education gets in the way of the entrepreneurial spirit— regardless of age.

I will also say that, based on a lot of years working with entrepreneurs, it is my opinion that MBA grads, in general, make poor startup entrepreneurs… even though there are a large number of people with advanced degrees in high-tech and finance.

Don't get hung up on age and formal education—they are not as important as you might think in starting a successful business. So, get started on that new business that is going to solve someone's problem—today would not be too soon!

5 • Fear of Failure

The late *Wilson Harrell*, famous entrepreneur and author, said that whenever an entrepreneur starts a business, especially their first business, they are automatically inducted into an exclusive club called the "Club of Terror." Harrell believed that entrepreneurship puts you in the grip of a human emotion that was created just for entrepreneurs.

Harrell calls this a "secret" club, because few entrepreneurs talk about their experiences in terms of "terror." But those who have experienced it (and most entrepreneurs have) know it is substantially more than just "fear of failure."

So, if you're suffering from fear of failure—or terror—you are not alone. Most aspiring entrepreneurs, as well as seasoned veterans of the business world are subject to fearing their business might fail.

On the other hand, if you think you will have smooth sailing when you start your business, you need to think again—you absolutely will have difficulties. And when your business starts to experience those difficulties, fear grows and can easily become the kind of terror that Harrell is talking about.

Carl Jung, the Swiss psychiatrist said, "Man needs difficulties: they are necessary for health." I'm not totally convinced of this... but if Jung is correct, there are a lot of healthy entrepreneurs around.

What is The Effect of This Fear?

Most business gurus and pundits maintain that lack of capital is the number one reason holding back many would-be entrepreneurs. But, since all new entrepreneurs — including the successful ones — face that same challenge, I believe that many people use lack of capital as an excuse for not starting their business... to mask their *fear of failure.*

From personal experience as an entrepreneur, business advisor, and consultant, plus considerable reading of research on the subject, I have concluded that *fearing they will fail* is the number one reason many people never start their own business.

So, before you give in to your fear of failure, consider this: "We should never allow our fears, or the expectations of others to set the frontiers of our destiny." — John O'Donohue, Author & Priest.

Can You Avoid The Fear of Failure?

I am frequently asked if a person can just start out part-time to see if their business "catches on," and to see if they like being an entrepreneur — avoiding as much fear as possible. This is quite like trying to wade across a cold river an inch at a time instead of just diving in... by the time you decide the water is o.k. the river has dried up, or you've lost interest in crossing.

Well, there are some instances where product development, or the like, could be done on a part-time basis. Or, you could start a small "side-hustle" business while you are learning about business basics and further developing your personal characteristics. But if your new business is to be your full-time livelihood, and fear of failure is holding you back, at some point you will need to go "all in" and face your fears.

When you reach that point; plan well—then act! Go fast; go hard—"You cannot blow an uncertain trumpet" (Theodore Hesburgh). If you nibble away at your plans, your fledgling business will never "get its legs" and grow like the business you envisioned—and it will likely whither and fail.

No, you can't entirely avoid Harrell's "Club of Terror," but there are ways to deal with the fear.

Dealing With Our Fear

Planning is the balm that will keep terror at bay... it won't eliminate it, but it will keep it from totally consuming you. As you go through your detailed planning for starting your business, you will identify things that could trip you up— issues you hadn't thought of before, and the fear and terror will begin to creep in. But, with good detailed planning that addresses those issues you can manage that fear.

For instance: You will make certain assumptions about the market for your product or service—but what if the market doesn't materialize? If this potential issue increases your fear level, you had better buckle down and do a more thorough job of market research... push away that feeling of terror with confidence in your planning.

Or... maybe when you start to build the Pro forma financials during your planning you suddenly realize that you don't really comprehend the whole aspect of "Pro formas" — and that terrifies you. That's a good indication that you had better learn more about financial statements, and their place in the business world before you proceed any further with your planning.

There are also other fear-fighting tools you can use to manage your fear, such as: training, knowledge, preparedness, awareness, decisiveness, and the like. These are the things that can turn fear into a motivator rather than a roadblock to your success.

The important thing to recognize is that you need to identify those things that bring on terror *before* they actually happen, and then you can take steps, using your fear-fighting tools, to minimize the feeling of terror when/if those things happen.

Will you catch everything that might bring on your fear while running your business? Not a chance. But by then you will have the experience of solving fear-causing problems, and every new issue will have less effect on you than the previous ones did.

Are You In The Grip of Fear?

I don't mean to sound cavalier about this; there is much to lose if your business fails — that is the risk all entrepreneurs take. But here's the thing: ***No one will boil you in oil if your business*** *fails!*

Also, here is something you may not have thought about. Even if your business fails, you will always take away all the benefits of working in a real-world situation and you will gain actual business experience that no MBA classroom or Harvard diploma could ever give you. While others were talking about entrepreneurship... you "experienced" it.

> *It doesn't matter how many times you fail. Each time only makes you better, stronger, smarter; and you only have to be right once. Just once... then everyone calls you an overnight success.*
> —Mark Cuban, Entrepreneur and Investor

* * * * *

There is only one Cardinal Rule when you are facing your fear of failure: you must remember that failure is an event, *not a* person. The only real failure in life is the failure to try.

I will leave you with this:

> *I really don't think life is about the I-could-have-been. Life is only about the I-tried-to-do. I don't mind the failure, but I can't imagine that I'd forgive myself if I didn't try.*
> —Nikki Giovanni, Poet and Teacher

6 • The Entrepreneur Gene — Fact or Fiction?

Over the years I've heard many people say things like; "Oh, I could never start a business — you need to be a born entrepreneur to do that, and that's just not me."

Or: "Boy, that guy is a born entrepreneur — every business he starts is successful. He certainly has the entrepreneur gene."

Could this be true?

The debate on whether business people are born with a special gene has been going on since before the term *entrepreneur* originated. One side of the debate stands firm that entrepreneurs are "born," not "made." The other side of the debate strongly maintains that anyone can become an entrepreneur if they want to.

I disagree with both sides of this debate — *somewhat!*

Certainly, if you read my report on business survival (get the report from my blog website bizmaverickblog.com), you could easily come to the conclusion that, because they fail so quickly, most new entrepreneurs should probably never have started a business in the first place. . Many business experts believe these businesses fail because the founders were not "born" entrepreneurs and therefore they are not capable of starting a successful business.

Yes, in many cases I'm sure people who should not, actually do start businesses. But I also do not believe that some people are *born* with a special gene that automatically makes them entrepreneur material... I think it is much more complex than that.

I look at the eight-year old who recently made $1.3 Million posting videos on *YouTube* and I wonder if this youngster has an entrepreneurial gene. Then I read in the *Kauffman Index* that the 55 to 64 age group is currently the most active age group for starting their first business. In one case the entrepreneur started very young, and in the other case it took many years before the older group became entrepreneurs. Why is that?

For some people, entrepreneurial characteristics seem to lie dormant and only develop and manifest themselves as the person grows and develops—perhaps over decades. I think for many people much depends on life experiences and ongoing training to develop their entrepreneurial characteristics.

Also, even though there *are* certain characteristics we are born with that might make becoming an entrepreneur easier for some—that is no guarantee for success. There are many people who appear to have all the characteristics of an entrepreneur, yet never have a successful business.

Don't just laugh this debate off as a bunch of meaningless hooey, because there are many people starting businesses every year that quickly fail—they should never have tried starting a business in the first place. They were just not prepared for it.

There is More to The Story

If people are *not* driven by a special entrepreneur gene, why don't more people start a business? There are many, many people who are stuck in a dreary job they hate, but don't believe they could ever leave their job and start a business.

Anyone who feels they couldn't start a successful business does not have the right motivation to be an entrepreneur, and obviously should not start a business — at this time. That doesn't mean they don't have the right characteristics of an entrepreneur... it might mean that many of those characteristics are lying dormant until later in life.

If you ever feel the nudge that you might like to start your own business at some point, here are some things you should try:

- ~ Visit the Business section of your local Library and look at some business books — ask for assistance from the Librarian.

- ~ Read some issues of *Inc.*, or *Entrepreneur* magazine and any other business magazines the Library might have.

- ~ If you have a *Kindle*, buy some basic *Kindle* business books that resonate with you.

- ~ Buy some basic print books from the Business section of *Amazon*, whether you have a *Kindle* or not. Use them for frequent reference.

- ~ Join a networking, or *Meetup*, group of people who are in a similar position as you.

~ Try to find a mentor or advisor to give you some one-on-one time to help steer you through your self-examination of entrepreneurship.

The thing you're looking for here is "motivation." Does any of this exposure to the workings of the entrepreneur's world excite you and make you want to get involved?

When entrepreneurial stirrings begin within you, that is the time to start investigating the possibilities and requirements of becoming an entrepreneur in more depth. You could even begin your very preliminary planning (see my *Primer Series* book *Small Business Planning: How to Plan Without Writing a Business Plan* http://amzn.to/1QpY80v)

Unless you already have a business background, this would also be the time to pick up some of the basic knowledge you are going to need to become a successful entrepreneur. Don't wait until you are up to your ass in alligators before you try to learn how to handle them.

Take some adult education business classes; spend more time with your networking or *Meetup* groups; search the Internet for information on starting a small business… and study as much business information as you can.

WARNING: There are many other attributes you need to check out before you make the final plunge to actually start a business and spend serious money. *There are some people who should never start a full-time business — even though they have the desire to do so.*

Also, many people move too quickly, before they are ready to be an entrepreneur. Most people who start a small business do not properly prepare themselves to become entrepreneurs. That is one of the main reasons over 5 Million businesses "disappear" each year in the U.S.

So, take a look at all the other considerations discussed in this book, and then give yourself the "Entrepreneur Test" in Chapter 8 to see if you really measure up to becoming an entrepreneur.

But first, let's take a look at the "Characteristics of An Entrepreneur" in the next chapter.

7•Characteristics of an Entrepreneur

As we discussed in an earlier chapter, the characteristics of an entrepreneur are developed early in many people. People who start early in life with lemonade stands, mowing lawns, running errands, etc. quite often continue their entrepreneurial endeavors through their school years and then emerge as an entrepreneur starting some kind of business.

Others may develop their entrepreneurial spirit later in life. They likely work at jobs through their early years to earn money for an education and then work at a good job with good companies. They usually don't appreciate entrepreneurship until much later, and probably discover their entrepreneurial characteristics gradually.

Does any of this sound familiar to you? Are you an aspiring entrepreneur—ready and willing to take on the risks of entrepreneurship? Or, is starting a business something you *think* you would like to do, but the idea seems somewhat daunting right now?

More important, how do you know if you (and your family) have the right stuff for you to be an entrepreneur?

Take a look at the following characteristics of an entrepreneur and pick out those you believe are your strengths, along with those where you could use more development. Be honest with yourself, this is not your test—yet.

Here then, are the characteristics of an entrepreneur:

Motivation —

Why do you want to be an entrepreneur? Since starting a business is extremely hard work and the prognosis for success quite low, why do you want to start a business? How motivated are you? Just because you lost your job recently is not necessarily a good reason — unless you have been thinking about starting a business for some time.

Are you a self-starter? Your motivation must come from within — there will be no one to give you direction, schedules, objectives, or assistance when you falter. You will have to motivate yourself to "do it all."

Turning negative things into further motivation is important. Can you take criticism as motivation? Again, how motivated are you?

Obsession —

This is a big step up from simple motivation. The highly successful entrepreneur Mark Cuban once said, "The first requirement of a person starting a business is that they must be obsessed." His second edict is that "If they have an exit strategy they are not obsessed."

Do you constantly think about starting your own business? Do you lie awake at night visualizing yourself running your business? Do you pass up that vanilla latte so you can put another few bucks into your startup fund?

This is an extremely important characteristic of an

entrepreneur and is where the wannabes are separated from the doers.

I want to be clear here. I am not talking just about your obsession with your business idea—I'm talking about your obsession to be an entrepreneur.

You need to be sure you can make a living at whatever business idea you have, but when that doesn't work out you need to maintain your obsession for entrepreneurship. This allows you to pivot on the fly and change your business idea, if necessary—or replace it altogether.

Are you beyond motivated? Are you obsessed?

Willingness to Learn—

Although just about every one in the business community has an opinion, no one really knows why around 5 Million businesses simply disappear every year in the U.S. (see *Business Survival Reality* report previously mentioned).

The majority opinion seems to be that most of these businesses were never "real" businesses in the first place and shouldn't even be acknowledged. So, if you start a business, and it fails, it appears that no one in the government or business community will even notice—or care.

For me, I would never say that your business doesn't matter—because it does! It matters to you and your family; it matters to your investors, creditors, and vendors; and it should also matter to the government and the business community at large.

On the other hand, I periodically receive requests for information on how to save a failing business. After a few initial questions, I usually ask them to send me a copy of their business planning, their Pro forma financial statements, and their actual financials to date... and I will take a look at their situation and offer some suggestions for recovery — for free!

And, I rarely receive the requested documents from these inquiries — *because they simply don't exist.* It also is apparent that, for the most part, they don't even know what those things are. It is true that you don't need a formal education in business, there are lots of ways to learn what you need to know as you "prepare and proceed" — but you *must* be willing to learn.

If you are not willing to learn how to start and grow a successful enterprise, then don't ever try to start a business, because you will fail.

Perseverance —

This goes hand in hand with your obsession and willingness to learn. Even though you may be obsessed, are you committed enough to stick with your dream through hard times; mistakes; plans that never materialize; elusive customers; employee problems; discouragement; long and longer yet hours; and the million things that can rise up and try to block your road to success.

Your passion will take a hit from time to time and that's when you need perseverance to push through the tough times (read about *John Mackey* and *Milton Hershey* in Chapter 13).

An entrepreneur must have certain attributes— perseverance being one of the most important.

Organization—

Successful entrepreneurs do not run around helter-skelter with a phone in one hand and a tablet in the other, trying to figure out how to get all the things done they think they need to do.

It is important to set personal goals and business goals, and then develop activities and habits that lead to the accomplishment of them. Only a strong organizational characteristic can make that happen.

Realistic scheduling; making lists (and following them); staying focused; managing your time; following your planning—these are all necessary organizational skills for the successful entrepreneur.

How do you measure up? Do you have what it takes to develop these skills?

Planning—

Perhaps this characteristic should be called "visualization," because you need to "see" in your mind how you want your business to operate. You need to visualize success and then be well enough organized to write down everything you need to do to achieve that success—in great detail.

It doesn't matter where or how you write your planning, you just need to write everything down. This is for your benefit—no one else may ever see this.

Unless you will be looking for investor capital, you do not need to worry about creating a "business plan." But, to imprint your thoughts on your brain, you do need to write down every detail about how you think you are going to make your business successful. Then as you gain knowledge and experience, and your planning needs to be tweaked, simply update what you have written—regularly.

Are you well enough organized to develop this information, and record it as you build your business?

Knowledge—

Do you have the core knowledge and expertise to successfully perform whatever activity your new business requires? Can you build, or oversee the building of your product or service? Are you specially trained to perform whatever service you intend to provide?

Some of this knowledge can be obtained as you go along,

but you do need some special knowledge and expertise about your product or service before you start. This is perhaps the most basic requirement of an entrepreneur.

How about your business acumen? You must have a basic knowledge of business. Are you willing to learn the general business basics you need to start and grow your business?

Fear of Failure —

Are you afraid you might fail? If your business failed, how would that affect you? Failure is a part of entrepreneurship. You will have ideas that fail. You will have projects that fail. You will have days where everything goes wrong. Your business may even fail! But, these are *events* — they are not you.

Thomas J. Watson Sr., founder of **IBM**, was once asked how to become more successful, and his response was. *"Have more failures."* Success is usually just one step beyond failure. Every entrepreneur has fears, but if you are going to become a new business owner, you will have to embrace your fears and rise above them.

Can you embrace your fears and not allow fear to stop you? For a more in-depth discussion on *Fear of Failure*, read Chapter 5 — over and over, if necessary.

Sacrifice —

Starting a business always requires sacrifices — at least initially. Can you make the sacrifices necessary to build your business? Can you completely change your lifestyle, and stop most current activities with family and friends because you will be working on your business instead?

It is easy to say you can, but it is quite another matter to actually do it. Think this one through very carefully, and visualize a life with few, if any, of your enjoyable activities for at least the short term — maybe longer.

Temperament —

Can you handle one frustration after another? This is important when dealing with all the people you will come into contact with while building your business. If your temperament is more like Seinfeld's "Soup Nazi," it would be better to not start a business where you had to deal with very many people.

Have you ever supervised employees? This is much different today than in the past, because expectations are different, and if you don't have the temperament to deal with difficult employee situations, you probably should not start a business that will require employees.

Be honest when analyzing your own temperament. What kind of an entrepreneur will you be?

Patience —

If you are going to be a successful entrepreneur, you must have the ability to wait for gratification. Becoming an overnight success might take several years.

Anyone thinking they will start a business and quickly make buckets of money is in for a rude awakening. Many of the 5 Million U.S. businesses that fail each year were likely started with the intention to provide quick money for the founder. If quick money is your motivation for starting a business—you will most likely fail.

Do you have the patience to go along with your perseverance, and not expect immediate gratification?

Risk Taking—

Becoming an entrepreneur requires taking risks. You will be risking money—yours and most likely others as well. Some people thrive on this type of risk, while others can't bear the thought of losing even a few hundred dollars.

How would you handle losing all the money you and your family invested in your venture? Could you? You also may be risking a steady well-paying job for an unknown future. No matter how much you dislike your current job—it does provide a regular income.

How risk averse are you?

Decision Making—

Are you a good decision maker? As a startup entrepreneur you will not have anyone making decisions for you. There will be a "million" things that require quick and incisive decisions to be made. You will need to make those decisions "on the spot."

Also, this is not just in the area of business issues you know about and are comfortable with. You will have to make quick decisions in areas of business where you likely have never had to make decisions before.

On a scale of 1 to 5, just how would you rate your decision-making ability?

Coping With Stress —

Starting a new business can be (and usually is) a highly stressful endeavor. So, how well do you cope with stress. Can you handle highly stressful situations without harming your health, or destroying your relationships?

Look back over your life-to-date and analyze those times that were very stressful. How well do you think you handled them? How did they affect you? Can you handle stress on a more frequent basis?

Selling —

The ability and drive to *sell* is one of the most important characteristics of an entrepreneur. Any small business owner/CEO of a small and growing business who cannot make sales calls, or participate in the selling process is unlikely to become a successful entrepreneur.

Whether you are selling products or services on the Internet, or hamburgers in your restaurant, you still must have sales, and you may be the only salesperson in your new business. Can you measure up? Do you love "selling?"

Flexibility —

Many people with good ideas become entrepreneurs and work very hard—only to fail. This often happens because entrepreneurship is not a linear process and very little goes according to plan. That is why the ability to be flexible is such an important entrepreneur characteristic.

If you can't change your thinking, your planning, and your business, quickly (often called "pivoting"), you will have a difficult time building a successful business.

How easy is it for you to adapt to change? Even to create change when necessary?

Family Support —

Of all the characteristics of an entrepreneur, this one is likely to be the most important. This is especially true if you have a spouse and children. You need to sit down and have a discussion with any and all family members that may be affected by your decision to become an entrepreneur.

How difficult will it be for you to have these discussions? Do you think you will get 100% support from your family, especially those that may be affected the most?

* * * * *

O.K., now that you've read all the Characteristics of an Entrepreneur—and have broken into a cold sweat—relax! If you aced every characteristic you would be considered perfect entrepreneur material... but rest assured that there are *no* "perfect" entrepreneurs. The important thing in this chapter is to identify those characteristics you are weak in and do everything you can to strengthen them. That is why a willingness to learn is so important.

There are thousands of web sites, hundreds of books, and dozens of people around you who can help with the technical stuff about starting your business — if you're willing to learn. But, no one other than you can provide the passion, obsession, perseverance — and all the other characteristics of an entrepreneur you need to achieve your dream.

Which of the above characteristics are you strong in, and which ones do you need to develop further? Before you answer too quickly, I suggest you take the "Entrepreneur Test" in the next chapter — then answer that question for yourself.

8 • The Entrepreneur Test

O.K., we've said that not everyone *should* be an entrepreneur, and that age and education are not determining factors. We've also talked about the nemesis of "fear of failure," and we have looked at the most important characteristics of an entrepreneur.

Now, it's time for you to determine if you have what it takes to become an entrepreneur. To assist you with this determination, I have created a simple test for you to self-administer.

Although I call this a "test," it is more of a guide for self-examination, because the answers are only important to you — not to anyone else. Also, this is not a "scientific" test, it is just an exercise for you to examine the questions and rate yourself against them... to determine what you need to do next to be an entrepreneur.

The test is straightforward — simply read each question and carefully consider how you feel about it. Then give yourself a rating from 0 to 5, with 0 meaning you don't feel you have that trait at all, and a rating of 5 meaning it's right down your alley.

Obviously, you can "game" this test by rating the questions in such a way that your total score shows up in the desired area. It is equally as obvious that, if you do that, you will have accomplished nothing, and you are wasting your time. Be honest with yourself.

Although there are a few similar questions, there are no trick questions and no negative questions — all questions can be positively rated from nothing (0) to a maximum of (5). Just remember to leave out your ego and pride when you rate each item — be as honest as you can.

If you're reading this on a digital device, you can simply use a piece of paper and write down your rating numbers in a column, then add up the column and compare the total to the scale at the end of the test.

Let's get started:

_____ 1. How would you rate your level of passion to become an entrepreneur (obsessed = 5)?

_____ 2. How willing are you to give up your current lifestyle — maybe for several years?

_____ 3. How comfortable are you at making new decisions on the fly — with no playbook, or manual?

_____ 4. How would you rate your track record for executing your ideas?

_____ 5. How well do you like cold-calling potential clients or customers?

_____ 6. How well do you always finish everything you start?

_____ 7. How well spoken and presentable are you?

_____ 8. How would you rate yourself as a self-starter?

_____ 9. How strongly is your significant other on board with your entrepreneurial idea? Will they support your desire to become an entrepreneur?

_____ 10. How successful do you think you would be at selling household products door-to-door?

_____ 11. How well do you accept rejection?

_____ 12. How would you rate your prior business experience—have you owned or run a business before?

_____ 13. How much formal business training do you have (none = 0 to MBA = 5)?

_____ 14. How good are your time management skills? Do you form good time management habits?

_____ 15. How sure are you that you can *mentally* sustain working 80-100 hrs/week for very long periods—if necessary?

_____ 16. How sure are you that you can *physically* sustain working 80-100 hrs/week for very long periods—if necessary?

_____ 17. How would you rate your flexibility—the ability to change plans and direction quickly when necessary?

_____ 18. How motivated are you to give back and share your wealth with others?

_____ 19. How afraid of failure are you (scared to death = 0 to no fear = 5)?

_____ 20. What is your level of resilience if your business does fail—can you immediately start another?

_____ 21. How determined are you in the face of obstacles? (Think "perseverance," not "stubbornness.")

_____ 22. What is your level of patience (it could take a long time to see success)?

_____ 23. What is your comfort level for taking risks?

_____ 24. How disciplined are your work habits? Do you stick to your self-imposed work schedules?

_____ 25. How good are you at taking advice?

_____ 26. How would you rate your organizational skills?

_____ 27. How would you rate your writing skills?

_____ 28. How would you rate your sales ability—are you experienced at selling?

_____ 29. How would you rate your public speaking skills?

_____ 30. How motivated are you by money?

_____ 31. How would you rate your willingness to bear great financial risk?

_____ 32. How would you rate your skill level at networking and building strategic relationships?

_____ 33. How would you rate your level of obsession with your new (or existing) product or service?

_____ 34. How willing are you to give up your current social life—indefinitely?

_____ 35. How experienced are you at analyzing financial statements?

_____ 36. How would you rate your marketing ability—do you have considerable experience?

_____ 37. How much technical knowledge do you have about your new product or service?

_____ 38. How would friends and family rate your entrepreneurial abilities?

_____ 39. How would you rate yourself as an extrovert? (Most people can't rate themselves accurately in this area, so ask for help on this one.)

_____ 40. How well do you handle long-term stress?

_____ 41. How well do you work with all kinds of people and personalities?

_____ 42. How much prior experience do you have as an entrepreneur? (None = 0, a prior successful business = 5.)

_____ 43. How would you rate yourself as an optimistic person?

_____ 44. How would you rate your experience in managing people (consider how many and for how long)?

_____ 45. How would you rate your planning ability — can you write a complete business plan?

_____ 46. How much do you enjoy hard work — for long periods of time?

_____ 47. How would you rate your level of competiveness?

_____ 48. Do you always complete all your projects? In a timely manner?

_____ 49. How good are you at managing money?

_____ 50. How would you rate your level of motivation for being an entrepreneur?

* * * * *

Now it's time to tally up all the ratings you gave yourself for each of the questions.

_____ Total Score.

Then, compare your total score to the following scale:

225 to 250 — Congratulations — great score! Unfortunately, that may not indicate that you are a prime candidate for entrepreneurship. You might have trouble finding the right business niche that matches your capabilities. So, I suggest you take the test again, but don't try to *game* the answers — you'll

only be fooling yourself. Then, if you think you were totally honest with yourself and still came up with a high score, you should read the section below titled "What If I Get a Very High Score? "

175 to 225 — You were probably not totally truthful with yourself yet and you should re-read each of the questions and try to imagine yourself in each of the situations presented — then re-take the test.

125-to 175 — This is the sweet spot in this exercise, because it signifies that you probably have the right stuff, but you also realize you still have a lot to learn and to experience about being an entrepreneur.

75 to 125 — Not too promising, but you may have been too hard on yourself. Why don't you wait a few days and take the test again — but stay absolutely honest, otherwise you will only be fooling yourself.

0 to 75 — Probably best that you keep your current job and build your career around it — and there is nothing wrong with that. Entrepreneurship is not for everyone; so don't try to force yourself into the role of entrepreneur "just because." (But, hang on; we'll look at this situation in more depth in the next chapter.)

* * * * *

Well, there you have it. Did you fully understand what is involved in each of the questions in this exercise?

If not, go ahead and take the test several times, if necessary, until you believe you have an honest answer to where you stack up as an entrepreneur.

Here's a suggestion: Have your significant other, or a family member, rate the questions on this test for you and see how close they come to matching your own ratings. Any ratings that are significantly different should be discussed between the two of you and resolved before you tally up the final score.

Of course, as I said earlier, there is nothing scientific about this self-test—it is merely an exercise to try and get you to apply some serious introspection into your own potential to become a successful entrepreneur.

Millions of businesses fail each year… you don't want to be one of them.

What If I Get a Very High Score?

Getting a high score in this exercise tends to put you in a rather special situation. That's why it's important to be as honest as possible when answering the questions. As mentioned above, you should consider having someone who knows you well work with you as you go through the questions again.

It's important to get this right, because here's what a very high score signifies:

~ You are an experienced manager of people.

~ You always finish projects you start.

~ You have considerable education in business.

~ You love selling and cold-calling — probably successfully.

~ You're a self-starter and willing to sacrifice your current lifestyle

~ You have probably had successful businesses in the past.

~ You're motivated by money and willing to take great financial risks.

~ You're well organized and have disciplined work habits.

~ You enjoy hard work with long hours.

~ You are a good planner and work well with people.

~ You take advice well and are a good money manager.

A very high score signifies at least the above attributes, and probably more — but hopefully you get the idea. A person with a really high score is probably not going to be satisfied starting and running a small business as a Sole Proprietor.

On the other hand, if you still have an obsession about becoming an entrepreneur, it may mean that you need to work with multiple partners, or a large team of professionals on a larger start-up project — a project where the company would keep rapidly growing and you could develop into a C-level position within the larger organization.

Here's another suggestion: Find a *Life Coach* to work with who can help you determine the direction you should take. It is a little known fact that most successful CEOs and company founders have coaches, mentors, or advisors of some kind that they can discuss those things with that are not for public knowledge. This is the small "shadow team" the public never hears about.

Then, if you, with the help of your shadow team, conclude that you should start a business, by all means get started!

In the next chapter, let's discuss what you might want to do if you feel you *failed* the test.

9 • What If I Fail the Test?

"If I get a very low score on the test can I still be an entrepreneur?"

First of all, the "Entrepreneur Test" is not a *pass-fail* test—it is simply a guide to help you determine whether or not you are ready to plunge into starting a successful business. "Failing" the test does not mean you *can't* start a business, it only indicates that you should spend some more time getting yourself ready before starting a business.

Getting ready could include anything from taking more classes, reading more books, working with a coach, starting some kind of "side-hustle" business—anything that gives you more education or insight into running a business.

So where do you start? With a low score on the test you have some work to do, probably both in the area of business education and in further development of personal characteristics. That is why, if you get a very low score, I usually recommend staying at your job while you strengthen your weaker characteristics and learn more about the business world.

Some Possibilities—

There are many successful entrepreneurs today who started out with a little side business that eventually grew into a major business... think: *Michael Dell* building computers in his dorm room after classes.

Many people start offering their services and knowledge on a small part-time basis from their home and then build their clientele up until they can quit their regular job and work full-time on something they love doing.

Another extremely popular side-hustle is starting a business on the Internet—making money online. I'm not thinking about the Internet millionaires that get all the media attention, but rather the many, many (no one knows *how* many) people everyday who are starting a small business on the Internet. They are not only constantly gaining more business knowledge, but they often make a little money on the side as well.

There are also many part-time Internet entrepreneurs who work long hard hours and finally build up their business to the point where they can quit their regular job and make a good living off the Internet. Unfortunately, not everyone can do this, because they can't relate to the "secret" of entrepreneurial success (see Chapter 10).

If you have a hobby you love, consider how you might use that to start a small part-time business. Some people make things and sell them at craft fairs—and this then turns into a small business. Others build (or have built for them) a website and they sell their, and/or other people's, products from that website.

Also, self-publishing books on *Kindle* and *Createspace* is still experiencing considerable growth right now.

The point is: If you are entrepreneur material, you have the ability to figure out a way to start some kind of part-time business to get you started while you learn the more intricate machinations of running a business. You are actually limited only by your imagination and passion.

Here are some suggestions on how to increase your business acumen and prepare yourself to start a business:

Education—

If you are still in school, take as many business classes as you can, especially those dealing with entrepreneurship. If you are no longer attending school, search out adult education classes on how to become an entrepreneur—any business class can be of value.

If you need to strengthen some of your personal characteristics, join *Toastmasters*, or a *Meetup* business group. There are also business-networking groups available everywhere. Learn everything you can from other entrepreneurs.

Just be careful you don't spend so much time educating yourself, that you never start your business.

Visualize—

If you want to become an entrepreneur you will need to cultivate and develop your ability to "visualize." You need to visualize how you would run the business of your dreams. At this point don't think about all the problems you could have—that can come later. To start, just see in your mind's eye the business of your dreams.

Also, do NOT think about startup money at this point. If you worry now about where the money will come from to start your business, you may never get started.

Talk to friends who have their own business and ask them how they decided to become an entrepreneur, and how they got started. Build on your vision while you are educating yourself.

Plan—

We talked about this before, but as your vision becomes clearer and details start falling into place, it will be time to start writing down your visualized plan for your business. This is NOT a "business plan," it is simply a compilation of your thoughts and ideas, and you can write them on the back of old envelopes if you want to… no one will ever see this planning except you.

This is perhaps the most important step when learning how to become an entrepreneur. Just be sure to concentrate heavily on where your customers are going to come from, and why.

If you want to study this concept of planning without writing a business plan, you can read my book on *Small Business Planning*. http://amzn.to/17ctulR

Money —

It is important that by some point you have a good handle on your money needs and you have Pro forma statements you can believe in (you will need to learn about these if you don't already know). With this done, you can incorporate your money needs and potential sources into your planning.

The vast majority of new entrepreneurs obtain their money from self, family, or friends. If you are going to start a larger business you may need to search for an outside Investor.

You can find more information on small business financing in my book titled *Small Business Bootstrapping: And Other Alternative Ways to Finance Your Small Business*. This is one of my *Primer Series* books and is available on Amazon. http://amzn.to/1Boyzn3

Prepare —

After your vision is fairly complete; your education is well along (you should never stop learning); and you have learned the basics of how to run a business; it is time to begin preparing for your new business.

You should also have a large portfolio, or notebook, of planning notes completed at this point, with Pro forma statements and a solid plan for marketing. This would be a good time to plan in more detail your pre-opening or pre-launch marketing activities.

Also, there are a myriad of other things you will need to do in preparation for starting your business—but you will have learned about these during your education activities.

Start—

With everything planned, prepared, and in place, the next step is to simply "start." Begin with the launch of your active advertising and promotion program. Potential customers need to know about you and what your business offers them that will fill their need.

Your planning and preparedness will, of course, coordinate this preliminary activity with the opening of your doors—physically or virtually, and the acceptance of customers.

Adjust—

No matter how much you plan and prepare, things will not go according to "plan." That is why formal business plans become obsolete almost immediately. But, your ongoing planning process can be quickly modified and adjusted according to what you experience early on in your new business. This is a very important requirement in your endeavor to become an entrepreneur, so don't skip over it.

* * * * *

I've only briefly touched on some of the steps you need to take to become an entrepreneur if you had a low score on your test. They may seem pretty simple, but don't take any of them lightly. Around 5 million businesses fail each year and it has been my observation that many of the failed businesses did not spend enough time and effort in these areas.

At the same time, if after reading these chapters on entrepreneurship and taking the test, you then decide that entrepreneurship is not for you... that's O.K. too—not everyone should be an entrepreneur. It's better that you find out early on.

I should mention that an entrepreneur with a low score on the Entrepreneur Test can often do much better than the entrepreneur with a high score... if they know and understand the *Secret* to business success.

If you rated a low score on your Entrepreneur Test, pay particular attention to the next chapter "A *Secret* to Entrepreneurial Success"—it just might be the thing that puts you ahead of the higher scorers.

10 • A *Secret* to Entrepreneurial Success

Yes, there is a *secret* to *successful* Entrepreneurship! At least, it must be a secret because so many entrepreneurs obviously don't know about it. And sadly, that's likely one of the reasons over 5 million businesses disappear every year in the U.S. alone.

Just what is this secret? Well, a few years ago a man by the name of *Ryan D'Agostino* struck out to learn about it. He wanted to find out why some people in America built fortunes, while others failed.

So, he decided to ask them.

D'Agostino used a list of the 100 richest zip codes in the U.S., visited 19 towns in 11 states, knocked on about 500 doors in these zip codes, and 50 people agreed to talk to him about how they became rich. When he finished his interviews he wrote a book titled "Rich Like Them." (It is available at Amazon, Barnes & Noble, and most other booksellers.)

This book is very informative and inspirational, but more interesting, there is a common thread (the *secret*) throughout all the interviews Ryan wrote about in his book.

Here are a couple of excerpts from Ryan's interviews. See if you can pick out this thread in these examples:

"I move $80 Million a year in produce, but you're only as good as your last load. The only thing that's kept me alive was knowing how to work hard. I may not be the smartest motherf[----]r in the world, but I can work harder than anybody." — Ted

"I work longer than most people because I think it's fun. I don't come home and watch TV at night. If you work twice as hard, you're going to be twice as successful." — Andy

These are just short samples from the 50, or so, interviews Ryan did. You can read the complete interviews in Ryan's book, but I think it's pretty obvious what this common thread through these interviews pertains to.

Here is what *D'Agostino* had to say about this:

"WORK HARD. Almost everyone I interviewed uttered those two words within their first few sentences."
— Ryan D'Agostino, "Rich Like Them"

And there you have the "secret." If you want to be successful, you will need to work hard *IN* your business as well as *ON* your business... regardless of what all the elitist business gurus and pundits try to tell you. If you want to be a successful entrepreneur you will *want* to work harder than everyone else.

The 4-Hour Workweek — Really?

Yeah, but what about the 4-hour workweek that best-selling author Tim Ferriss talks about in his book? Well, if you read Tim's book carefully, you will learn that he worked 15-hour days until his business became successful enough to start hiring people to take over part of the day-to-day operation.

In fact, Tim Ferriss worked himself into a nervous breakdown before he was convinced he needed to hire some help.

I periodically receive questions from people just starting out in business and they are looking for a shortcut, or simple solution, to business success. They seem to take offense when I tell them they need to learn business basics, have a great idea, and then *work their ass off.*

Just keep in mind: *Working ON your business, not IN your business* is the worst possible advice anyone could give (or take) for the entrepreneur about to start a business. When you're just starting a new business, you *will* work IN your business — *or you will fail.*

Does that mean you will have to work 80-100 hour-weeks for the rest of your life? Of course not — unless you want to. As you grow and become increasingly successful you will need to gradually work more on strategies and new ideas (ON your business) while others you bring in can start to take over the day-to-day operational work.

But, being an entrepreneur doesn't stop there. Even Tim Ferriss pointed out that working a 4-hour workweek on his business does not mean he only works 4 hours a week on *business*. Tim said in his book that he works almost as many hours per week on new ideas and new projects (he built the *4-Hour* concept into a successful brand) as he initially did on his main business.

O.K., so we all know now that we have to work hard to get a business started — and to make it successful — so, what is the bottom line here?

The Bottom Line

If you want to avoid the failure trap that around 5 Million businesses in the U.S. fall into every year, it is imperative that you seriously — very seriously — consider the following issues before you ever commit to starting a business:

~ Are you obsessed with becoming an entrepreneur? REALLY obsessed?

~ Do you have a truly great business idea — one you are passionate about?

~ Are you prepared to give up your life as you — and your family — know it?

~ Regarding the above item, give serious thought to all the time you spend watching TV; using your electronic gadgetry; participating in sports and hobbies; spending time with your friends; spending time with your family; and all the things you do today that you will not do, or do much less of, after you start your business?

~ Do you have the willingness to learn all the things about business you will need to know to have a successful business?

~ Can you follow the "secret" to being a successful entrepreneur and work the long hours it takes to get a business firmly started

and growing? How long could you work this hard?

~ Can you work through bouts of frustration, sickness, despair, exhaustion, terror, etc.?

~ And most important – do you think you have what it takes to become a successful entrepreneur… can you be an entrepreneur?

Study the earlier chapters, especially; "What is an Entrepreneur?" "Why Be an Entrepreneur?" and "Characteristics of an Entrepreneur," then be sure to take the "Entrepreneur Test." Read again this chapter on the *secret* of entrepreneurial success to see if that is something you could embrace.

If you shrug off these things as just so much rhetoric to fill a book – you will fail when you start your business… along with 5 million other people who didn't pay attention.

11 • The Home Business Entrepreneur

I included this special chapter on home businesses, because **69% of all U.S. entrepreneurs start their business at home.**

Many of those entrepreneurs who start in their home eventually move to more formal business quarters, but many businesses that are started in the home remain there... for the life of the business.

Also, if you are only looking to start a small "side-hustle" business, you will likely start it from home. You can then work part time and make a little money on the side... or work on developing a product or service for a full time business in the future.

There is certainly nothing wrong with starting your business at home. Steve Jobs and Steve Wozniack started *Apple* in Jobs bedroom, and then moved to his garage when the bedroom got overcrowded. That arrangement seemed to turn out all right.

Perhaps the most extreme case is John Paul DeJoria—his home was his car. John Paul started *Paul Mitchell*, with a business partner, while living in his car and selling products to hair salons out of the trunk of his car. DeJoria is now on the Forbes list of the richest men in the U.S.

I could go on and on, but the point is; unless you need a busy storefront location for walk-in customers, you don't need fancy business surroundings to become an entrepreneur. In fact, it is much better if you start out as lean as possible. Don't waste precious capital on personal trappings around you.

Types of Home Businesses

There are three basic types of home businesses. The first is the business that is started in the home where the entire operation of the business resides in the home — for some indefinite future. This includes most small online businesses like Internet marketers, website designers, authors, etc.

This works well as long as your business stays small, but as a business grows it might eventually require additional facilities.

The second type is the business that uses their home as a base of operation and the entrepreneur performs their work somewhere else, like a plumbing business, personal shopper, electrical contractor, insurance agent, some forms of professional services, etc. Again, as the business grows, perhaps more equipment or inventory is acquired, or employees are added — then this type of business might need to add facilities.

And the third type of business is where the early planning and startup stages occur in the home with the full intention to move out as soon as the business gains some traction, like Anita Roddick, Sarah Blakely, Bette Nesmith Graham, and many others (see chapter 13, "Famous Entrepreneurs").

Most entrepreneurs start up with little or no money, so costs must be kept to an absolute minimum. A spare bedroom, basement, garage, or just the kitchen, furnished with thrift store desks, files, and office equipment will work just fine at the beginning.

Now, let's look at some of the advantages and disadvantages of most home businesses.

Advantages of the Home Business Entrepreneur

Many of the advantages are pretty obvious, such as; no additional overhead costs for facilities, no immediate additional childcare costs for those with young children, close proximity to your business whenever you have a few moments to work on it, and on and on.

You can also save a great deal of time (and money) by eating a quick meal just a step away from your desk or workbench.

Every entrepreneur has a somewhat different situation, but getting your business started at home almost always simplifies the early stages of planning and preparation, if not your entire operation.

If you will need it, you probably already have high-speed Internet service in your home—or it can be easily upgraded. And, unless you need heavy machine tools, or other special equipment, you likely already have most of the things you need to start your business in your home office.

Disadvantages of the Home Business Entrepreneur

Probably the greatest, and most common disadvantage of the

home business arrangement is that you never get away from the "office." It is always right in front of you—psychologically and physically.

There is always that tugging feeling to just step over a few paces and do one last thing you just remembered; or to take a look at your email or Facebook page; or a hundred other little (or big) things you can't mentally, or emotionally, get away from… because you are still "in the office."

Then, perhaps, the next biggest disadvantage is the expectations of members of your family. There might be children to take to school and pick up after school. You want your kids to share their day with you, but not when you are in the middle of a conference call or webinar presentation, or trying to meet an important deadline.

Family members expect the house to be kept clean, the shopping to be done, and meals prepared on time. This is not a gender thing—it is expected of you because you're "home" all day.

The same is true of friends and family outside the home. They all know you are home, so they don't think twice about calling you, or stopping by for a cup of coffee and a chat. They don't do it maliciously, but most people have little understanding of what it means to be a home business entrepreneur.

This is where it becomes necessary for you to be a strong disciplinarian—both to yourself and to outside distractions. If you're going to have a successful home business, you must set a rigid schedule for yourself, and be a downright hardass about outside distractions.

* * * * *

So, being a home business entrepreneur has its advantages and its disadvantages. Low cost and available facilities on the plus side, and frequent disruptions on the negative side.

But, millions of entrepreneurs make this home business thing work, and it simply can't be beat as a low cost way to get your business started.

12 • The Facts About Internet Entrepreneurs

Let's be clear—this chapter is not about having a website for your business and using it to promote your business. Every business today should have an online presence... it is the billboard, and *Yellow Pages* of yesterday.

I'm also not talking about people who amassed great fortunes building services that are used *on* the Internet, like; *Google, Twitter, Yahoo, LinkedIn, Facebook, Instagram,* and on and on.

What this chapter deals with are the everyday business entrepreneurs who use the Internet—on an exclusive basis—as their virtual office, store, or warehouse. They conduct all of their business through their online capabilities—they are *Internet Business Entrepreneurs.*

These Internet entrepreneurs might just be the hottest growing segment of the small business world today. It is hard to escape the ads, the unsolicited emails, the articles, the books, etc. that come across our screens every day, extolling the financial wonders of becoming an online entrepreneur.

We also hear much about "Internet Millionaires" and how easy it is for you and I to become one. This is usually from those who make their millions by telling other people how to become extraordinarily successful as an online entrepreneur—if they buy their courses, books, coaching, and so on.

I have been studying the online business world since it first started and I have concluded that there are four types, or levels, of Internet entrepreneurs, as follows:

Level 1 — The True Online Millionaire

These are the top-level online entrepreneurs who have been extremely successful using the Internet over some period of time. Many of this class of entrepreneur have created high-revenue corporations that employ many people, and/or retain a number of freelancers for outsourced work. Many of the people at this level make millions of dollars per year, so I arbitrarily put those making $1 Million or more into this group.

The main thing that bothers me about this category of Internet entrepreneur is that most of them make their millions by selling products and services that are supposed to teach other people how to become online millionaires.

This creates an industry "churn" that appears almost incestuous. At best, the products and services offered by these millionaires function in a similar manner as multi-level marketing — the more people they draw into their sphere of influence, the larger their potential customer base, and profit, becomes.

But, it obviously works… many people become millionaires by telling other people how to become millionaires.

Level 2 — Pre-millionaire Internet Entrepreneurs

This is the group that has not quite broken the million-dollar annual revenue number, but yet has been quite successful in building an online business. I put businesses into this category that have annual revenues in the $250,000 to $1 Million range.

They do basically the same things as the millionaire group, but haven't been at it as long, or have not been as successful. People in this category may be your best source for teaching and coaching online beginners — if that is what you're looking for.

Level 3 — New Upcoming Internet Entrepreneurs

This is, by far, the largest legitimate group and is where all Internet Entrepreneurs start, so this group has annual revenues between $0 and $250,000. This is the level where you create your first product or service, and begin trying to attract new clients or customers.

Many people within this group make very little money, and very few ever achieve the higher end of $250,000. Still, some achieve a nice standard of living and have little desire to build a larger business enterprise.

You need to be careful working with anyone in this group, because there will be many people trying to sell you something that is supposed to make you rich, while they themselves have made very little.

Regardless of whom you decide to learn about Internet

entrepreneurship from, be sure to check them out thoroughly before you pay them any money.

Level 4 — Pure Evil!

This is the level that I lump all the scammers, spammers, hackers, blackmailers, pornographers, etc. into. These are the people who create the websites and schemes that use unethical (often illegal) means to extract money from naïve people who use the Internet.

Unfortunately, it appears that this might be the fastest growing segment of online businesses. Scams and spam top the list of bad behavior on the Internet and very few people who use the Internet escape the workings of this group.

Anyone considering starting an online business of this nature need not read this book, because they are more criminal than entrepreneur and they will find little information of value to them here. I strongly encourage you to steer clear of anyone in this group. There are no free lunches and no Internet streets paved with gold — be very careful.

* * * *

Those are the levels of Internet entrepreneurial activity as I view them. Others may categorize them somewhat differently, but I think you probably get the idea.

There are however, some common considerations that apply to all the prior levels of entrepreneurial activity, and they are something you should clearly understand, and take into account before you embark on trying to become an Internet entrepreneur.

Let's take a look:

Poor Success Rate —

Very few people actually make a lot of money by selling things on the Internet. The general consensus seems to be that somewhere between 2% and 4% of people who try Internet businesses actually become successful. Very few ever reach Level 1 today.

It takes a special promotional type of person to make it really big on the Internet, and most people are just not that type.

No Free Lunches —

Most people fail at becoming a successful Internet entrepreneur because, not only is it very hard work, it often takes a long time. Most "Internet millionaires", when pressed, will tell you they worked at it for a long time — and made many mistakes — before they started to make a *lot* of money.

Making money while you sleep may work for the established Internet entrepreneur, but don't expect to be able to do that for quite some time — if ever. Sadly, it is the specter of hard work that causes many people to fail at having a successful business on the Internet.

"Opportunity is missed by most people because it is dressed in overalls and looks like work." —Thomas Edison

Hype, Hype, Hype—

There is so much hype online about how you can start an Internet business and become rich quickly, that the *FTC* has to step in from time to time to try and control some of the blatant false claims that are being made.

The first rule for becoming an Internet entrepreneur is to NOT believe the hype—the claims of many people who have really not made a big success of their Internet business. For the most part, these people are predators who prey on the uninformed and those who read about (and believe) all the millions of dollars that can be made quickly by starting an online business.

Unfortunately, there is no quick, easy, and effortless way to become an entrepreneur—even an Internet entrepreneur.

Financial Investment—

In order to achieve a high level of success on the Internet, you will have to make *some* financial investment. First of all, you should have the basic business knowledge that any other entrepreneur needs.

Then, you will need a decent computer system. A 10-year old laptop likely won't get you very far. Your system does not have to be state-of-the-art, but it does have to be good enough to get the job done.

You should also have a high-speed Internet connection, and although they are not outrageously expensive, they are an ongoing expense. If you only have dial-up service available, you will have to be more selective about the type of business you get into.

And, of course, you will need your online business presence—a website. This will be your storefront, office, classroom, or whatever, and it could be quite expensive. If you are highly capable, perhaps you can build it yourself, or you can outsource the job. Just be aware that high quality ecommerce sites can be costly.

Also, you will likely have to pay for some form of special Internet business training, and some advertising—which may increase as your business grows. You may also need to buy some books and guides. All startups require at least *some* money.

So, that is the hard side of being an Internet entrepreneur. But, there is a tremendous bright side as well, so let's take a look at the potential of Internet entrepreneurship.

Opportunity...

Make no mistake; if you have the characteristics of an entrepreneur, and are capable of developing focus... plus have a willingness to work very hard over a long period of time... you could join the small elite group of successful Internet entrepreneurs—the small 2% to 4% of all those who attempt it.

Even at that low success rate, that is a lot of people. Six-figure incomes (or more) are possible in this group of people, and if you can make it into their company, you will do very well indeed.

Probably the greatest advantage to this kind of business is that although you need some money to get started, it is usually a small amount compared to what you might need to start up a more traditional business. Just about every online business is started in someone's home, and the majority stays there for the life of the business.

Can An Introvert Be An Internet Entrepreneur?

This is a very complex subject with no good answer. First of all, there are several different types of Introverts, and it is not the intent of this book to delve deeply into the matter.

But, I'm asked this question every once in a while, and I tell those folks that it is probably possible to find some kind of little known, but highly active, niche that is populated with people just waiting for you to come along and fulfill their needs.

Unfortunately, this situation is not common and the typical high-income online entrepreneur is almost always an extrovert with enough sales pizzazz to successfully sell used cars or vacuum cleaners door to door.

Making money online normally requires a great deal of promotion. Introverts are usually not very good at self-promotion, and that is something you will just have to overcome.

I have read articles by millionaires where they state they are introverts and shy—but yet, they travel around the country (or world) giving keynote speeches, putting on workshops, creating weekly or daily podcasts, giving webinars and interviews, and functioning as kings and queens on social media. This doesn't come naturally to introverts—but it can still be done.

So, from what I observe, if you are truly an introvert, unless you are an expert with some kind of special capability, you will have a great deal of difficulty becoming an Internet millionaire.

That does not mean that you cannot make a good living online. If you have something to offer that fills a need, and a means to get that information to the people who have the need, you can still make a good living as an online entrepreneur.

There are good and bad sides to being an Internet entrepreneur, but if you understand what an entrepreneur is, have the characteristics of an entrepreneur, and are willing to work very, very hard at it—you too could become an Internet Entrepreneur.

So... Do it! —

Whether you start slowly until you get your feet wet, or go for a major launch right away, will depend on the area you are going to concentrate on and the knowledge you bring to your business.

Since starting a business on the Internet is basically little different than starting any other new business, I recommend you pay close attention to the chapters in this book—and also take the "Entrepreneur Test."

But, whatever you do, don't get hung up in research and planning to the point where you never get around to starting the real work. Set a deadline for starting your business and stick to it... or, definitely decide against becoming an entrepreneur.

13 • Famous Entrepreneurs

When today's young business owners think of famous entrepreneurs they immediately think of people like Bill Gates and Paul Allen (Microsoft), Jeff Bezos (Amazon), Steve Jobs and Steve Wozniack (Apple), or Larry Page and Sergey Brin (Google), and similar others.

These certainly are celebrity entrepreneurs — they (and many others like them) are today's famous entrepreneurs. But, what about those entrepreneurs who blazed the trails for today's entrepreneurs? How many business students, or MBAs for that matter, know much about **Adam Smith**?

That he is widely acclaimed as the father of modern economics — better known as *capitalism.*

Adam Smith was born in Scotland in 1723, and without his magnum opus *The Wealth of Nations,* we might have a very different view today of free enterprise and free markets. Adam Smith could easily be considered the first of a long list of famous entrepreneurs — starting in 1723.

Listing all the famous entrepreneurs in the world would take many volumes, so I am going to present only a few of my favorites. I want to concentrate on some of those who started their business with little, or nothing, and bootstrapped their way into entrepreneurial success — and may, or may not, have achieved worldwide recognition.

But, I have also included a few well-known names in the mix, because there are some facts about them you may not be familiar with.

Have a look at the following:

Anita Roddick

Although the late Anita Roddick was a well-known businesswoman, I have included her here because she was one of my all-time favorite entrepreneurs. Anita started with absolutely nothing; failed at a couple of businesses; and then she bootstrapped her last business into one of the most successful cosmetics companies in the world.

She began by mixing skin lotions in her kitchen... borrowed money from the corner gas station owner... and became one of the most well known entrepreneurs in her generation. In 1993, she was knighted by the Queen of England, and given the title of *Dame Anita Roddick* for her entrepreneurial success.

Adam Osborne

Born in Thailand of British parents, he began his career by writing and publishing easy to read technical manuals. He sold his publishing business for several million dollars and created the first portable computer — the "Osborne I."

Adam is credited with being the first computer manufacturer to bundle application software into his computer. He also sold that model computer for half the cost of desktops already on the market.

Osborne went into hyper growth and was shipping 10,000 computers per month at the peak. He was not prepared for this kind of growth and quickly went bankrupt.

We can learn from people's failures as well as their successes.

Madame C.J. Walker
Born Sarah Breedlove, she became the first female millionaire entrepreneur. Walker was the daughter of former slaves, and an orphan at age seven.

She was in her 30's when, working with her brothers, who were barbers, she developed her first hair care products. From there she built a highly successful beauty products company, and employed over 3,000 people at its peak.

Simon Cowell
Best known as a talent judge on the TV show *American Idol*, and a highly successful (and wealthy) music producer. I included him here because he is lesser known for producing the show for new entrepreneurs: "American Inventor."

Mary Anderson
Few people know that Mary Anderson invented the automobile windshield wiper, and received her patent in 1903.

Debbie Fields
Although her name is also well known, it is not so well known that she once was an Oakland Athletics "ball girl" making $5 per week so she could buy cookie ingredients.

Debbie started her business at age 20—with no previous business experience—and she built it to 730 stores in 11 countries. She sold her company to a private investment group, but remains the spokesperson for the company.

Henry Ford

To set the record straight—Henry Ford did *not* invent the automobile. Nor did he invent the assembly line.

He did, however, along with his management team, perfect the application of the assembly line, as well as the concept of using interchangeable parts on automobiles.

Ford built the first mass-production auto plant and paid the highest wages in the industry—$5 per day. A worker there could buy a new Ford car for the equivalent of less than 3 months wages.

Ford also had several failed business attempts before he tried building automobiles.

Mary Kay Ash

Mary Kay Ash founded "Mary Kay Cosmetics" at age 45, with $5,000 invested by her son. Ash formed her company on the principle of the *Golden Rule* and she advocated praising people to success.

Her company was included in "the 100 best companies to work for in America," and was named the "Most Outstanding Woman in Business in the 20th Century," by Lifetime Television.

Harvey Mackay

Best known as a motivational speaker and author... Harvey started his career in high school by selling subscriptions door-to-door, cutting grass, shoveling snow, and clerking in a men's store.

Following college, he worked as a salesperson for an envelope company and when he was 26 he purchased an insolvent envelope company with 12 employees. Today, his envelope company employs over 500 people and has annual revenues over $100 Million.

Patricia Billings

Artist, inventor, great-grandmother... Billings developed a product called Geobond© which is a perfect replacement for asbestos in construction. The last I heard, Billings turned down a reported $20 Million offer for her secret formula.

Ingvar Kamprad

Not a name you often see in today's business media; Kamprad is the founder of "IKEA." He started out in business by selling matches to neighbors, then fish, Christmas decorations, seeds, and pens and pencils.

He founded IKEA at his kitchen table when he added furniture to his product line.

Today he is generally regarded as one of the richest men in the world, and he also flies coach, takes the subway to work, and drives a 20-year old car.

Michael Dell

A well-known name, but I included Michael here because he started his entrepreneurial career by selling newspaper subscriptions door-to-door while in high school (he made more money than some of his teachers).

He later started "Dell Computer Corporation" in his dorm room at the University of Texas, with just $1,000.

He became the youngest CEO in history to head a Fortune 500 company, and is now reported to be one of the wealthiest men in America.

Bette Nesmith Graham

Graham was a secretary who wanted a better way to correct typing errors in film-ribbon typewriters and multi-colored carbon forms. She experimented at home in her kitchen and developed a product she called "Mistake Out," later renamed "Liquid Paper." She sold her company to Gillette for $47.5 million.

Margaret Knight

Ms. Knight is the inventor of the machine that manufactures the paper bags we see—and use—in grocery stores. Knight founded the "Eastern Paper Bag Company" in 1870.

She also created over 100 inventions (including a rotary engine) and obtained around 26 patents. She was once described as a "woman Enstein."

Wayne Huizenga

Wayne is the only person in history to have founded three Fortune 500 companies... one in waste disposal, one in video entertainment, and one in auto sales. He also owns the "Miami Dolphins."

Sarah Blakely

Sarah is the youngest self-made female *billionaire*. Working at menial jobs in Florida, including selling fax machines door-to-door, she disliked wearing pantyhose while wearing open-toed shoes, because of the seamed toe area. And, when she cut the foot off, the pantyhose rolled up her legs.

As a result, with little money, and working out of her apartment, she created the product "SPANX." Sarah is the sole owner of the company, which is now worth over a Billion dollars.

In 2014 she was ranked the 93rd most powerful woman in the world by Forbes magazine.

John Paul DeJoria

John was 36 years old and living in his car when he started selling hair products out of the trunk of his car. He borrowed $300 from his mother to buy inventory and started cold calling on hair salons across the country.

Today he is on the Forbes list of the 100 richest people in America.

John Mackey

When John Mackey was 25 and his girlfriend Renee Lawson was 21, they raised $45,000 from family and friends and opened a small organic grocery and vegetarian café in an old Victorian house. They had a one-room office on the top floor, which they also lived in, sleeping on a foldout futon couch. The first year they lost $23,000, and they struggled with cash flow problems for the next 14 years.

Obviously, their perseverance and struggles paid off, because their business grew into "Whole Foods Market" with over 400 locations, 87,000 employees, and over $14 Billion in annual revenue.

What if John and Renee had given up after that first disastrous year... or any time during the first 14 years of financial struggle—including being completely wiped out by a flood and not having any insurance? Passion... obsession... following their dream? You Bet!

Milton Hershey

Born on a farm in Pennsylvania, Milton dropped out of school at the age of 13. When he turned 14 he apprenticed with a confectioner and four years later he borrowed $150 from his aunt and opened his own candy shop in Philadelphia. The business quickly failed.

Milton worked for other confectioners and then again started his own candy shops in Chicago and New York. They too were failures. He finally went back to Pennsylvania and started the "Lancaster Caramel Company." This business was finally a success. Hershey later sold that business to buy the new German equipment that allowed him to perfect the now famous "Hershey" chocolate.

Hershey was perhaps the most philanthropic businessman of his day and he built an entire town around his chocolate business. But, what if Milton Hershey had given up after his first business failure… or his second… or his third? So often, success is just around the corner from your last failure.

Ruth Wakefield

You'll love this person—Ruth Wakefield is the inventor of the "Chocolate Chip Cookie." Ruth and her husband purchased an old building that was once used as a roadside tollhouse, and converted it into an Inn called the "Toll House Inn." Ruth cooked meals for guests, and word of her food, and especially her desserts, quickly spread.

One day she had to substitute broken pieces of "Nestlé's" semi-sweet chocolate for cocoa powder in her "Butter Drop Do" cookies… and the "Toll House Chocolate Chip Cookie" was born. "Nestle" later made a deal with Ruth, putting her recipe on their package of chocolate bits, in exchange for a lifetime supply of chocolate. (Not all successful entrepreneurs become millionaires.)

* * * * *

It is interesting to note that most of these famous entrepreneurs were not products of the *Internet,* or the digital revolution. With few exceptions, these people saw (or found) a need for something, and then filled that need. That is the simple formula for entrepreneurial success.

14 • Entrepreneur Quotes

Thousands of quotations inspirational to entrepreneurs can be found in various sources, but some are more helpful and beneficial than others.

So, for this chapter I have selected several quotations that have been meaningful to me over the years.

New entrepreneurs need all the inspiration they can get, and I think the following quotations will provide some of that for you:

I have a dream. *– Martin Luther King*

Do not be concerned that you might set a target too high and fail. Be concerned that you will set it too low and succeed.
– Michelangelo

The critical ingredient is getting off your butt and doing something. It's as simple as that. A lot of people have ideas, but there are few who decide to do something about them now. Not tomorrow. Not next week. But *today*. The true entrepreneur is a doer, not a dreamer.
—*Nolan Bushnell*, Founder of Atari and Chuck E. Cheese's

Don't be afraid to take a big step. You can't cross a chasm in two small steps.
—*David Lloyd George*, Former Prime Minister of England

I never perfected an invention that I did not think about in terms of the service it might give others... I find out what the world needs, then I proceed to invent. — *Thomas Edison*

If you can dream it, you can do it. — *Walt Disney*

It is not the employer who pays the wages. Employers only handle the money. It is the customer who pays the wages.
— *Henry Ford*

Capital isn't that important in business. Experience isn't that important. You can get both of these things. What *is* important is ideas. — *Harvey Firestone*

A friendship founded on business is better than a business founded on friendship. — *John D. Rockefeller*

I had to make my own living and my own opportunity! But I made it! Don't sit down and wait for the opportunities to come. Get up and make them!
— *Madam C.J. Walker*, First female entrepreneur to become a self-made millionaire

Genius is 1% inspiration, and 99% perspiration.
— *Thomas Edison*

Dot the i's, cross the t's, answer the phones promptly, send out errorless invoices, and in general never forget that the devil is in the details. — *Tom Peters*, Business Guru

The key is to just get on the bike, and the key to getting on the bike... is to stop thinking about 'there are a bunch of reasons I might fall off' and just hop on and peddle the damned thing. You can pick up a map, a tire pump, and better footwear along the way.
—*Dick Costolo*, Founder of *Feedburner.com*

The important thing is not being afraid to take a chance. Remember, the greatest failure is to not try.
—*Debbi Fields*, Founder of *Mrs. Fields Cookies*

Execution Excellence! (Show up on time! Leave last!)
—*Tom Peters*, Business Guru

Opportunities magnify as they are seized. —*Sun Tzu*

To achieve anything, you must be prepared to dabble on the boundary of disaster. —*Stirling Moss*, Grand Prix racer

The healthiest competition occurs when average people win by putting in above average effort.
—*Colin Powell*, Former Secretary of State

No great marketing decisions have ever been made on quantitative data. —*John Sculley*, Former *Apple* CEO

There is no man living that cannot do more than he thinks he can. —*Henry Ford*

The first responsibility of a leader is to define responsibility. The last is to say thank you. In between the leader is a servant.

—*Max De Pree*, American entrepreneur and author

Don't ever let anyone tell you that something is too competitive. Once you subtract the people who don't work very hard, or the people who aren't as good as you, your competition shrinks dramatically.

—*Maggie Mason*, Founder of *Mighty Goods*

Business has only two basic functions—marketing and innovation. —*Peter Drucker*, Writer, Management Consultant

Life is really simple as far as I'm concerned. There is no luck, you work hard and study things intently. If you do that for long and hard enough you're successful.

—*Jason Calacanis*, Founder of *Weblogs, Inc.*

If you want to increase your success rate, double your failure rate. —*Thomas J. Watson, Sr.*, Founder of *IBM*

The best reason to start an organization is to make meaning; to create a product or service to make the world a better place.

—*Guy Kawasaki*, Venture capitalist

It doesn't matter how many times you fail. It doesn't matter how many times you almost get it right. No one is going to know or care about your failures, and neither should you. All

you have to do is learn from them and those around you because all that matters in business is that you get it right once. Then everyone can tell you how lucky you are.
— *Mark Cuban*, Founder of *HDNet*

However beautiful the strategy, you should occasionally look at the results. — *Winston Churchill*

I find that when you have a real interest in life and a curious life, that sleep is not the most important thing.
— *Martha Stewart*, Entrepreneur and Business Personality

Remember: You are the only human being in the world who can help this particular customer at this particular moment in time. — *Tom Peters*, Business Guru

Obstacles are those frightful things you see when you take your eyes off your goal. — *Henry Ford*

Tap into people's dignity, and they will do anything for you. Ignore it and they won't lift a finger.
— *Thomas L. Friedman*, Pulitzer Prize-winning author

Experience taught me a few things. One is to listen to your gut no matter how good something sounds on paper. The second is that you're generally better off sticking with what you know. And the third is that sometimes your best investments are the ones you don't make.
— *Donald Trump*, Entrepreneur/Investor

Most people live and die with their music unplayed—they never dared try.
—*Mary Kay Ash*, Founder of "Mary Kay Cosmetics"

I have always found that my view of success has been iconoclastic: success to me is not about money or status or fame, its about finding a livelihood that brings me joy and self-sufficiency and a sense of contributing to the world.
—*Anita Roddick*, Founder of "The Body Shop"

Organizations exist to serve. Period. Leaders live to serve. Period. —*Tom Peters*, Business Guru

A business that makes nothing but money is a poor business.
—*Henry Ford*

It is not enough that we do our best—sometimes we have to do what's required. —*Winston Churchill*

Challenges are what make life interesting; overcoming them is what makes life meaningful. —*Joshua J. Marine*

If everything seems under control, you're just not going fast enough. —*Mario Andretti*, professional racecar driver.

Chase the vision, not the money; the money will end up following you. —*Tony Hsieh*, Founder of *Zappos*

Half the game is 90% mental.
—*Yogi Berra*, baseball player and philosopher.

Be not afraid of going slowly, be afraid of standing still.
— *Chinese Proverb*

Before anything else, getting ready is the secret of success.
— *Henry Ford*

Be the best. It's the only market that's not crowded."
— *George Whalen,* author and retail expert.

Vision without action is a daydream. Action without vision is a nightmare. — *Japanese Proverb*

You need more than passion — you need an intensity that will scare people. — *Ryan D'Agostino*

In every success story, you will find someone who has made a courageous decision. — *Peter F. Drucker*

* * * * *

Well, there you have a few of my favorite inspirational quotations from some pretty successful people. Of course, there are hundreds more of these relating to business and entrepreneurship that can be found on the Internet.

When there seems to be just too many roadblocks in your business, I believe it is often helpful to take some time out to read some of these famous quotations and visualize how they might apply to your situation at the moment. Give it a try — it might make all the difference.

15•So... Can I Be An Entrepreneur?

Well, after reading this book, what do *you* think? *Can you be an entrepreneur?* The fact is—you are the only person on earth who can answer that question. Your "shadow team" around you can give their opinions, but you are the one who has to make that final decision.

I've tried to give you some tools to help you through the process of doing some insightful analysis, but you have to do the analysis yourself—no one can do it for you.

Whether you think you are ready to be an entrepreneur, or you still have a few concerns, here is what you need to review:

~ Are you clear on why you want to be an entrepreneur? Are you obsessed with becoming an entrepreneur?

~ Do the issues of age or education concern you? If so, you should re-read chapter 4—these are not really issues at all.

~ Do you have enough business knowledge to successfully start and run your business?

~ How great is your "fear of failure?" Is this an obstacle, or is it something you can readily overcome?

~ Do you think you have enough "characteristics of an entrepreneur" to be a successful entrepreneur?

~ How did you score on your "Entrepreneur Test?" Do you have a plan for improving those areas where you scored low?

~ Can you embrace the "secret" of successful entrepreneurship and make the commitments and sacrifices required of every successful startup?

You need to have confidence in your responses to the above questions, and if you have any "pause" on any item you should work on that area before trying to start a business.

Before anything else, getting ready is the secret to success.
—Henry Ford

Of course anyone *can* start a business—but not everyone *should.*

My concern is that every year in the U.S. we see over 6 million people starting full-time businesses... along with over 5 million people who don't last long enough to file an income tax return.

We may be entering the *age of the entrepreneur,* and that is great for many people... but it is not the be-all and end-all of the business world.

There are thousands of self-made millionaires around who are not entrepreneurs, and never were. Being an entrepreneur is more about personal freedom, taking control of your life, and making the world a better place.

I hope you took the "Entrepreneur Test" to see if you thought you had the prerequisites to become an entrepreneur. Remember, this is not a scientific test; it is simply a guide to help you with your own analysis of your readiness to plunge into the world of the entrepreneur.

If your test results indicate that you are probably not ready to be an entrepreneur, it only means you have some more homework to do before you try starting a business. It's better to wait while you build up your capabilities than it is to jump into a situation you may be sorry for.

In the final analysis, only you can determine if you have all the necessary characteristics, capabilities, and resources to become an entrepreneur.

Hopefully, this book can help you examine the various aspects of being an entrepreneur as they may affect you personally. The intent is to give you the insight you need to make the right decision about becoming an entrepreneur… or not.

So, you need to make the final decision, and if you decide to be an entrepreneur… then do your homework; make your preparations; and launch that business so that one day your name can be added to the list of "Famous Entrepreneurs" … and everyone can tell you how lucky you were.

About the Author

Bob Foster's background spans a few decades. It is also unusually eclectic in that it includes working with the smallest of small businesses as well as Fortune 100 companies.

Bob has worked as CEO or consultant at businesses from the high-tech world of the "Silicon Forest," to the commercial fishing grounds of Alaska and Mexico.

He's worked on projects involving products from beer to computers, and in industries from pulp and paper to urban renewal.

Along the way Bob earned a reputation for saving businesses that were deemed unsalvageable.

He started businesses and sold businesses, and was lied to by large multi-national corporations (according to the late *Wilson Harrell*, all big corporations lie). As an entrepreneur, he felt the excitement of success as well as the sting of failure.

Even though Bob spent part of his career working for large corporations, it is the small business arena that excites him — where Entrepreneurs are born and flourish.

So, that is the foundation and background upon which Bob is now sharing with entrepreneurs everywhere — what he learned from real experiences, not just in classrooms.

Contact Page

Email Contact: bob@bobfoster.biz

Bob's Resource Site: www.bobfoster.biz

Bob's Blog: www.bizmaverickblog.com

Business Information website: www.business-solutions-and-resources.com

Note—

If you're still struggling with the idea of becoming an entrepreneur, I invite you to send me your concerns or questions in an email at the above address, and I'll try to help you with any issues you may have.

Becoming an entrepreneur is not something that should be approached lightly... having a business fail is a good learning experience, but having a successful business is even better.

Bob Foster